Around the Churches *of* **The South Hams**

Walter Jacobson

with love —
Walter

OBELISK PUBLICATIONS

Also by the Author

Around the Churches of East Devon
Around the Churches of Exeter
Around the Church of The Teign Valley

Other Books About this Area

The South Hams in Colour, *Chips Barber*
Walks in the South Hams, *Brian Carter*
Around & About Hope Cove and Thurlestone, *Chips Barber*
Around & About Burgh Island and Bigbury Bay, *Chips Barber*
Around & About Salcombe, *Chips Barber*
Newton Ferrers and Noss Mayo, *Chips Barber*
The Great Little Totnes Book, *Chips Barber*
The Ghosts of Totnes, *Bob Mann*
Walks in the Totnes Countryside, *Bob Mann*
The Ghosts of Berry Pomeroy Castle, *Deryck Seymour*
Place-Names in Devon, *Chips Barber*
An A to Z of Devon Dialect, *Chips Barber*
Haunted Pubs in Devon, *Sally and Chips Barber*
Ghastly and Ghostly Devon, *Sally and Chips Barber*
Murders and Mysteries in Devon, *Ann James*

We have over 170 Devon-based titles; for a list of current books please send SAE to 2 Church Hill, Pinhoe, Exeter, EX4 9ER or telephone (01392) 468556

Acknowledgements
All photographs supplied by Walter Jacobson and Chips Barber.
Front cover of Ermington Church and back cover of Wembury Church by Chips Barber.

First published in 2001 by
Obelisk Publications, 2 Church Hill, Pinhoe, Exeter, Devon
Designed and Typeset by Sally Barber
Printed in Great Britain

CONTENTS

INTRODUCTION

When Chips Barber suggested that I follow up my series on Devon churches with a book on the South Hams, I had only a vague idea of what was in store. Previous visits to Dartmouth and occasional walks along the most beautiful coastline imaginable were no preparation for the delight I was to find in making a detailed survey of the unspoiled countryside south of the Exeter–Plymouth road.

Roads, mostly narrow and winding, go up and down hills through glorious Devon, and suddenly out of nowhere there appear long-settled villages, always with a church tower or steeple conspicuously at the centre, or on rises overlooking the settlements, like guardians keeping a constant watch over their citizens.

And the traveller is always aware of the rivers that have carved valleys out of the hills as they move on "to espouse the everlasting sea".

The buildings themselves, always lovingly preserved (although often vast in proportion to the populations they serve), are packed with fascinating stories of the past – as witnesses of Viking and cross-Channel invasions, as the last homes of prayer for departing Crusaders, and most recently as venues for meetings to plan the evacuation of 3,000 people from six parishes in 1943–44 to enable American troops to prepare for the Normandy landings.

The names of Raleigh, Gilbert and Davis and seafarers over the centuries have close associations with the churches and their communities, and from Dartmouth along the coast to Salcombe and then on to Wembury I was constantly reminded of the poet's words: "The hollow oak our palace is, our heritage the sea".

Towers and steeples of the coastal churches, too, have had their part to play, standing as beacons to sailors seeking the havens where they would be, symbolising the truth that all these loved places are faithful guides to those who live near and to every passer-by.

Aveton Gifford Church

ST PETER'S CHURCH, UGBOROUGH

STANDING above the village square on a site which was once believed to be an earthwork fort, St Peter's is a large building – somebody has measured it as 131 feet long.

Much of the surrounding parish can be viewed from the sturdy 94-foot turreted west tower made of Dartmoor granite. The high moor itself can be seen reaching up to the north; to the west is the wooded valley carved by the River Erme on its way from the moor to the sea; to the east is a green rolling landscape, deeply indented by the Avon, another major river of the South Hams.

The main structure of the church dates from the 14th century, but the fine, though damaged, Norman font of red stone is evidence of an earlier building.

Wealthy Royal favourite Lord William Brewer, who lies buried in his own Dunkeswell Abbey in East Devon, acquired Ugborough Manor at the end of the 12th century, and with its income endowed another of his foundations, Torre Abbey, "with one ferling of land in Uggburgh and with common land of Dartmoor".

The church, however, belonged to Plympton Priory, and the first known Rector of Ugborough was Hugh de Plympstone, instituted 1266.

Fine bosses in the north aisle include one of a sow and eight piglets – the symbol of St Brannock, the Irish saint who came from Wales in the 6th century to convert the people of North Devon. Another boss depicts St Loye (or Eloys), the patron of blacksmiths and goldsmith to King Dagobert, mentioned in Chaucer's *Canterbury Tales*.

A memorial to Thos. Williams of Pyke is a reminder of a double link with the neighbouring parish of Harford, on Dartmoor, in the Erme valley. Williams was the son of Thos. Williams, Speaker of the House of Commons in 1563, who is portrayed in armour in St Petrock's, Harford.

When young John Prideaux, also of Harford, was turned down for the job of parish clerk at Ugborough, a sympathetic patron gave him a scholarship to Exeter College, Oxford, where his outstanding work earned him a chaplaincy to James I and also his appointment as Bishop of Worcester, all because – he was wont to explain – of his rejection at Ugborough.

Among other outstanding interior features of the church, whose exposed high points outside make eerie music out of the north winds blowing from Dartmoor, is the 17th century pulpit carved out of stone.

Pictures painted by a Jacobean artist – 32 in all – adorn the panels of the screen with a variety of subjects, including St Sebastian being pierced by the archers' arrows, St Apollonia (who intercedes for those with toothache), and St Dorothea (her emblem a basket with roses and apples).

The nave, which in its present form has welcomed worshippers for almost seven centuries, has no seating in part of its spacious west end, and on the stone ledge around the wall there is an explanatory notice. It aids the imagination to a glimpse of the past: "The old stone seats are supposed to be a survival of the days when there were no seats in the body of the church – the congregation standing or kneeling on the earthenware floor, the seats against the wall being provided for the aged and the infirm."

ST PETER AND ST PAUL'S CHURCH, ERMINGTON

TWO Devon churches – at Ermington and Barnstaple – are famous for their crooked spires. The 3-foot westward tilt of the late 15th century steeple of St Peter and St Paul, Ermington, may have been caused by the use of unseasoned timbers, but a more romantic version is that soon after it was built, the 100-foot steeple stretched its neck to get a better view of a beautiful bride, Miss Bulteel, entering the church.

There is some indication that a wooden church was built on the site in Saxon times, a belief supported by the fact that Ermington gave its name to one of the Saxon "hundreds" established over a wide area of the South Hams for administrative and legal purposes. O. J. Reichel's *Domesday Churches of Devon* also mentions a Saxon building here.

The manor of Ermington passed from Edward the Confessor to William the Conqueror, and Henry I bestowed it on the Peverell family, who probably built and cared for the first Norman church. Richard Peverell (1259) is the first listed rector.

The family gave the Priory of Montacute in Somerset the tithes and advowson (the right to appoint clergy), and in the Middle Ages it seems that three clergy were employed – a chantry priest, a rector (often an absentee), and a curate who actually looked after the parish.

An ancient tomb in the south chapel catches the eye. It is associated with the Strashleigh family, who occupied Strashleigh Manor from the 13th century until 1583. By marriage, first the Chudleighs, and later the Prideaux family, acceded to the property. A fine Elizabethan brass, now kept in the vestry, depicts William Strashleigh (died 1583) at prayer with his wife Anne and their only daughter, Christia, the future wife of Christopher Chudleigh.

The most remarkable features of the church interior, however, are the works carved by the daughters of the Rev Edmund Pinwill, who was appointed vicar in 1880, and stayed for nearly 50 years. The seven daughters, who are listed on a wall memorial, were sent by their mother to learn their art from a master craftsman. A striking example of their skill is immediately visible on entry into the building. It is the reredos Nativity scene on the main altar, shaped in alabaster by Miss Violet Pinwill, the most talented of the sisters, who worked on with her own staff in a Plymouth studio until her retirement in 1954, fulfilling orders to adorn many Devon churches. The pulpit was carved by Violet at the age of 17. Bench ends, chapel screens, and font cover are other examples of the sisters' work.

A clergyman who visited the church 150 years ago, before it was so beautifully restored, wrote: "Some helmets were lying around. I tried one on, and it was a most uncomfortable piece of headgear." It is worthy of note that two of these ancient helmets of unknown origin are now secured on the wall of the south chapel.

ST GEORGE'S CHURCH, MODBURY

MODBURY parishioners are rightly proud of their magnificent church dedicated to St George. Its mediaeval spire, floodlit by night, rises 134 feet on a hill above the market town, and can be seen from great distances across the South Hams.

Lofty, light, spacious, and well preserved by church members, the interior is also full of interest for visitors with a love of history, aided by the excellent, up-to-date guidebook.

On this site a church – one of 50 in Devon at the time – was recorded in the Domesday Survey. After the Conquest the squire, Rainald de Vallentorta, founded a small Benedictine priory dependent on the Abbey of St Peter sur Dives in Normandy.

Modbury priory was dissolved by Henry VI in 1442, and the revenue from its lands endowed the new Eton College at Windsor. Dean Milles' Parochial Returns of 1755 record: "There was an alien priory in the time of Henry V of which nothing remains, now wholly converted into a field, the freehold belonging to Eton College since its foundation."

Valletort Manor passed by marriage into the hands of the Champernownes, one of the two great families who for centuries dominated local history. Their memorials are in the south transept of the church. In the north transept are the effigies – mutilated by Cromwell's men – of the Prideaux family of Great Orcheton.

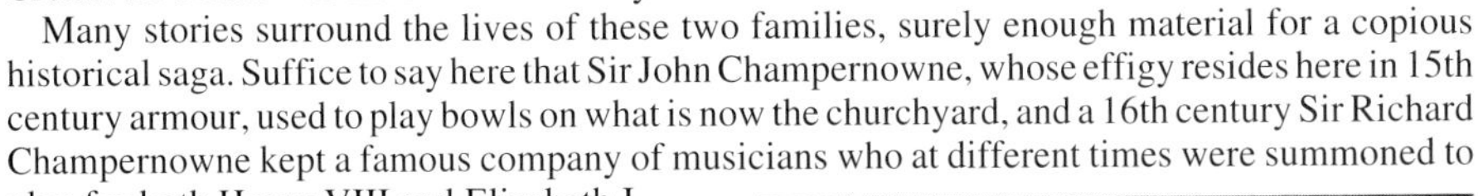

Many stories surround the lives of these two families, surely enough material for a copious historical saga. Suffice to say here that Sir John Champernowne, whose effigy resides here in 15th century armour, used to play bowls on what is now the churchyard, and a 16th century Sir Richard Champernowne kept a famous company of musicians who at different times were summoned to play for both Henry VIII and Elizabeth I.

Katherine Champernowne, of Modbury House, who married first Otho Gilbert, of Compton, and secondly (when widowed!) Walter Raleigh of East Budleigh, was mother of three great Elizabethans in English seafaring history – Sir Humphrey Gilbert, Adrian Gilbert and Sir Walter Raleigh.

Thirteen generations of the Prideaux family at Orcheton produced a number of county sheriffs, including Sir John, sheriff in 1383, who according to an old legend "slew his relation Sir William Bigbury, in a place called Five Crosses near Modbury." May Heaven preserve the present peace of the South Hams!

The ring of six bells now in the tower was subscribed by parishioners in 1806 and cast by Thomas Bilbie of Cullompton. They have been described as some of the finest in the diocese. The Church Goods Commissioners of 1553 recorded the four bells then in use, which probably were originally cast for the priory, as "being of Norman origin and exquisite in tone". Perhaps it was these bells which first inspired the local rhyme:

Hark to Modbury bells, how they quiver;
Better than Ermington's down by the river.

ST ANDREW'S CHURCH, AVETON GIFFORD

A SCENE of unassailable peace was presented in Arthur Mee's description of Aveton Gifford (pronounced Awton Jiffard) just before the Second World War: "A village of the old world prettily set among the hills. From the hill by the church we have a fine view of the Avon, curling along the last miles of the journey to the sea."

Five years later, on 26 January 1943, the peaceful scene was shattered by German fighter bombers in a raid which killed one little girl, injured 20 people, and left the church, the rectory, and 10 other homes in ruins.

Still in use in the restored St Andrew's Church, however, is the ancient granite font, which was toppled but undamaged by the raid. A tablet in the porch records the official re-dedication of the building by Bishop Robert Mortimer of Exeter on 12 October 1957.

First Lord of the Manor of Avetone was Ruald Adobatus, "dubbed a knight by the Conqueror himself", who ended his life in St Nicholas Priory in Exeter.

Were the Giffards, who later held the manor and probably built the first Norman church, his descendants? There is a clue that this might be so, in that the other 'Giffard' parish – Weare Giffard in North Devon – was also held by Ruald in 1086.

An effigy of Devonian Walter Stapeldon above the lectern recalls that in 1308, when he was already Bishop of Exeter (1308–26), he was also Rector of Aveton Giffard.

It is possible that Stapeldon never visited Aveton Giffard (although its revenues helped his income), but the parish remains proud of its connection to one of the leading English churchmen and statesmen of his time. Before his murder by a London mob in 1326, he founded Exeter College at Oxford, and was chaplain to Pope Clement V and Lord Chancellor to Edward II. He also started the rebuilding of Exeter Cathedral.

There are records of two 15th century bequests to the church. The first was £2 from the will of John Whytloff, Rector of Loddiswell, "for work then in progress" (he also left similar sums to five other churches in the Woodleigh Deanery). By her will of 1407 Isabella Danmarle asked to be buried in the church and left £100 for its upkeep – a huge sum in those days, perhaps almost matching in real terms the £30,000 from the War Damage Commission needed to repair the damaged building in 1957. It preserves much the same cruciform shape as its original Norman design.

Rector William Lane won renown in 1643 organising local people in a brave but unsuccessful attempt to halt the Roundhead Army as it crossed the Avon bridge to take Modbury. The Rev Benjamin Vaughan ministered here for 57 years until his death in January 1847 in his 87th year. Baptised in St Andrew's in 1790 and trained in his craft as a mason by his father in the village, Robert Macey walked to London and set up business in Fleet Street and is remembered for building several churches, hospitals, and theatres, including the Adelphi and Haymarket.

Pleasing features of the rebuilt church are the east and west windows contributed by Marion Grant and the altar provided by the Women's Institute.

ST MARY THE VIRGIN CHURCH, CHURCHSTOW

WITH views in every direction over the surrounding countryside, St Mary the Virgin Church, Churchstow, has occupied its prominent position for a thousand years or more. It was first established as an oratory of the manor of Notona (or Norton), which had been bestowed as a gift to the Abbot of Buckfast in the Domesday records of 1070. The tower, made like the rest of the building from local slate, can be seen for miles around.

This was an important place from early times. A 1274 record discloses: "At Churchstow, which the Abbot of Buckfast holds, there are gallows and an assize of bread, beer, and ale."

It was also the mother church of the area, overlooking Kingsbridge, which was a new borough carved out of the Norton manor lands by Buckfast Abbey (c.1220).

An abbey appointee, Rector Roger Bachelor, in his will of 1417 bequeathed "shepe and kine to the store of the Blessed Virgin Mary and also two marks for the repainting of the image of the Virgin in the chancel."

When the abbey was dissolved, the manor and church advowson (along with many others) were acquired by the wealthy Petre family. Sir William Petre, of Torbryan, was Secretary of State to four successive Tudor monarchs – Henry VIII, Edward VI, Mary, and Elizabeth I. The line of his descendants, the Lords Petre, has survived to our own times.

A relation, John Peters esquire of St Thomas, Exeter, bequeathed to Churchstow (as he did to other South Devon churches) "20s a year in fee forever for the releave of the poor". Perhaps it was through his influence that the right to appoint clergy to Churchstow and Kingsbridge was acquired by the Mayor and Chamber of Exeter. This was transferred in the 20th century to the Bishop of Exeter.

The spacious south porch affords a pleasant welcome to the building, which is well lit by the early 16th century south aisle windows. There is a Jacobean pulpit, and evidence of the age of this centre of worship, as may be expected, abides with the square Norman font bowl.

A local entry in *The Devon Village Book*, compiled by the Devon Federation of Women's Institutes, thankfully records: "In February 1988, the church tower was struck by a thunderbolt, but the lightning conductor saved the building."

A mile from the church, at the Domesday manor of Leigh, a fine gatehouse was built by a cell of Buckfast monks who lived there. It is still known as Lower Leigh Austin Priory. Restorative work on the gatehouse was helped by English Heritage.

ST ANDREW'S CHURCH, EAST ALLINGTON

HOW a Fortescue led Norman cavalry charges at Hastings, had three horses killed under him during the battle, and placed his shield between William the Conqueror and certain death is part of the nation's romantic history. His descendants played a big part subsequently in Devon and English history, and St Andrew's, set high on Church Hill at East Allington, contains several Fortescue memorials.

The family became established in the parish in the early 15th century when Sir Henry Fortescue, Lord Chief Justice of the Common Pleas in Ireland, married a de Fallaputte heiress, and so acquired Fallapit House, which the family retained until the 19th century.

Of two Tudor brasses, one commemorates John Fortescue (died 1595) and his wife, Honor; the other shows a kneeling woman, thought to be Elizabeth, wife of Lewis Fortescue who was one of Henry VIII's Barons (judges) of the Court of Exchequer. A floor stone is in memory of Edward Fortescue, Sheriff of Devon in 1624, and his wife Mary Champernowne. More recently a family memorial was carved by Sir Francis Chantrey, leading sculptor of his day, his masterpieces including the statue of King George III in the London Guildhall.

When the Fortescues sold Fallapit to William Cubitt, he helped restore the church in 1875 with a gift of £2,500. He was a member of the famous family of engineers and architects who were responsible for the 1851 Great Exhibition building.

Other notable features of the church are the 16th century screen and the pulpit, with eight armorial shields of Fortescues at its base.

There is a 19th century account of how the church had four different fonts in the course of a decade. An attempt was made first to restore a "crude" old Norman font, which had been ejected earlier and was in use as a pig trough, but it broke in transit. Its replacement, a small specimen, was eventually considered unsuitable and given to a mission chapel in the area. Its successor, a larger font of "free stone", was in turn replaced in 1899 by an alabaster font carved by Harry Hems of Exeter, given in memory of the Rev Henry Fortescue (54 years rector). Water damage to the alabaster, however, soon rendered it unusable. Finally a font of Devon marble was provided.

Descending the steep hill from the "wildflower-friendly" churchyard of St Andrew's, it is time for travellers to take refreshment at an inn – where else but at the aptly named Fortescue Arms!

ST MARY THE VIRGIN CHURCH, DIPTFORD

A CLOCK records the right time in one of the few mediaeval broach spires left in Devon, adorning the Church of St Mary the Virgin, Diptford. It stands tall, overlooking its village, a broad stretch of rolling countryside, and the steep descent to the River Avon.

It must have been a worshipping centre for well over a thousand years, because Diptford was the meeting place of the Saxon Stanborough Hundred, administrating a wide area stretching along the Avon down to the coast.

The Domesday name of Depeford also clearly indicates the parish's significance as a crossing point over the Avon, and "Bickham Bridge" is mentioned as early as 962 in a charter of King Edgar.

A Crown manor and church advowson was acquired by William the Conqueror on the death of Edward the Confessor. Henry II bestowed these rights on Reginald, Earl of Cornwall, and Risdon records: "Diptford was an ancient inheritance of the old family of Mules and descended to the Earl of Huntingdon." Such landlords built and cared for the Norman church, and the present nave arches were already in place when Bishop Grandisson dedicated the high altar on 14 June 1336.

The most celebrated rector to hold office here was Dr Barnabas Potter (also Vicar of Dean Prior), who became Bishop of Carlisle in Charles I's time.

Edward Nosworthy, appointed rector just after Charles II was crowned in 1660, remained here for the next 59 years, spanning the reigns of four Sovereigns.

The splendid condition of church and churchyard today makes it hard to visualise what the building was like in 1848, when an Exeter Diocesan report described it as being "in a woeful state of dilapidation – the chancel is destroyed."

Symbolic of the parishioners' devotion to the church in recent times is the glass case of memorabilia of postmistress Cicely Elizabeth Fanny Clapp, of Star House, Diptford, who was organist and choirmaster for 60 years. The display includes the British Empire Medal awarded to her in 1979 for outstanding services to the community.

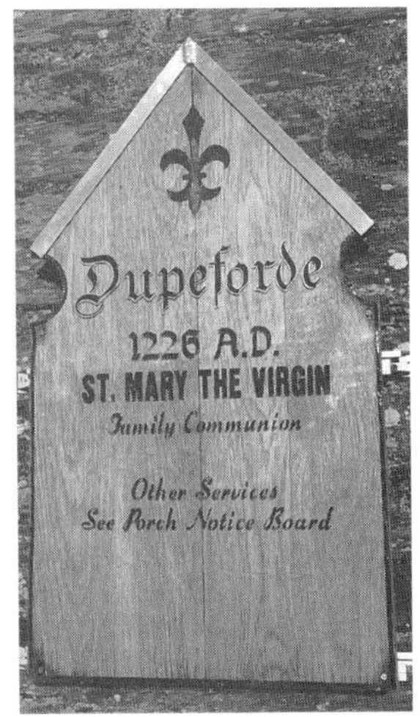

The names of more than a hundred men of the parish are recorded on a memorial as having served their country in the Great War, and on the walls of the screened bell-tower are numerous certificates for ringing awards.

The lane is lined with wildflowers as it descends from the village, crosses the Avon Bridge, and ascends the hill opposite to St Mary's Church, North Huish, which is also crowned with an octagonal mediaeval spire.

It has a fascinating history of its own; suffice to mention here that the rector from 1705 to 1759 was John Cross, whose claim to fame was his expulsion from Magdalen College, Oxford, for refusing to vote for James II's choice as college president.

The two churches, with their twin spires, stand like sentinels in the east and in the west, both perpetually blessed with breathtaking views down the valley of the ever-flowing Avon.

ST MICHAEL AND ALL ANGELS CHURCH, LODDISWELL

ON the hilltop about two miles to the north of Loddiswell are the remains of prehistoric earthworks, which, on a site later adapted into a Norman fortress, are known locally as The Rings or Blackdown Camp. One legend claims that the most recent skirmish took place there nearly 900 years ago, during a campaign when the three sons of King Harold came over with a force from Ireland in a vain attempt to win back their father's throne. When Judhael, Lord of Totnes, was awarded Loddiswell lands by William the Conqueror, he arranged for the first Norman chapel to be built at the head of the sheltered valley where exotic plants and a vineyard now thrive.

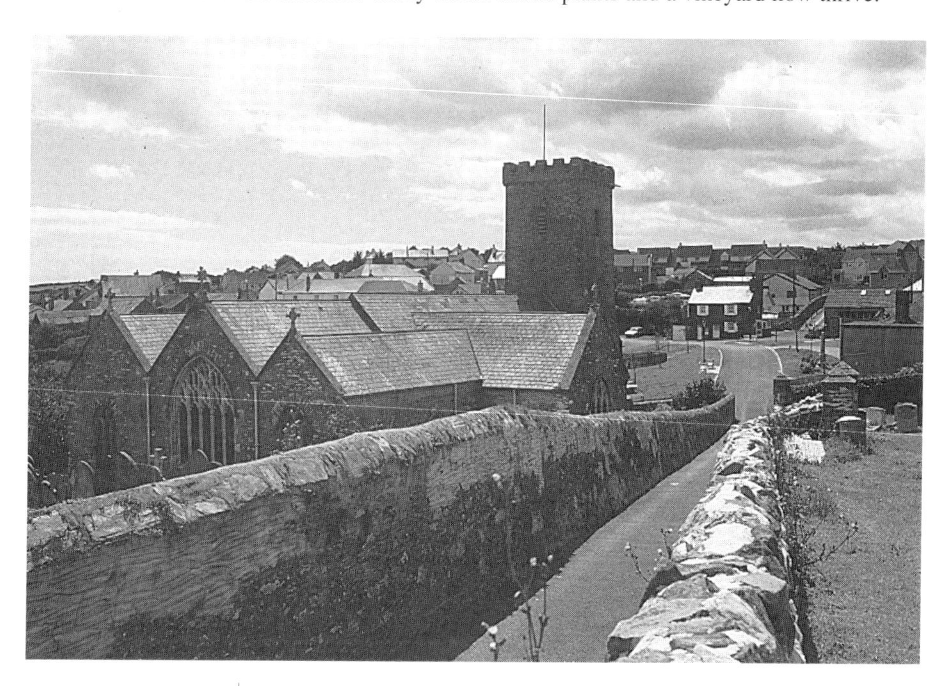

The 14th century Church of St Michael and All Angels retains the unique redstone font handed down from those days. Transeptal arches were also part of an earlier Norman structure, and a north window still displays some mediaeval stained glass.

The north aisle is sometimes known as the Woolston chapel, where the Furlongs and later the Wises, of Woolston Manor, worshipped, were buried, and placed their memorials. For some centuries the care of the building must have been largely in their hands.

The bearer of another famous West Country name, Sir Matthew Arundell, in 1591 established a charity which has benefited the community over the years.

Richard Peek (1787–1867) of Hazelwood, a parishioner who went to London in his youth, made a fortune out of tea, and has his memorial in a pulpit given by his relatives. It is inscribed: "After rising to high estate and offices in London (he was appointed the city sheriff in 1832) he returned to his native parish, where for many years he was a respected and honoured magistrate and a wise and tender friend of the poor." The Peek family in 1988 made a gift of The Rings camp and fort as a place of recreation for the people of Loddiswell.

Each year on St Stephen's Day (26 December) the wishes of another benefactor, Richard Phillips, are fulfilled. Under his will, the elderly of the parish are invited to stand on his tomb in the chancel and receive gifts of cash from the chairman of the Loddiswell Feoffees.

ST EDMUND'S CHURCH, KINGSBRIDGE

SHIPS may no longer need St Edmund's Church as a landmark to bring their cargoes into the Kingsbridge Estuary, but it makes an impressive spectacle to welcome visitors approaching the ancient borough from land or sea.

From the market established by the Abbot of Buckfast in 1219, the town grew in status to become a borough in 1238. One source claims that the name Kingsbridge is derived from a charter of 962 which refers to a bridge linking two Royal estates – Chillington in the east and Alvington in the west.

This explains the rare dedication (in Devon) of the parish church to St Edmund, the English King who in 869 was defeated by Danish invaders and took refuge under the arches of a bridge. Subsequently "bridge" chapels were named after him, including one in Exeter, now a ruin, beside the remains of an old bridge over the River Exe. A chapel was first built on the Kingsbridge church site in the 13th century. An undated deed discloses that "The Rector of Churchstow, Magister de Litelcombe, permits the Abbot of Buckfast to erect a church in honour of the Blessed Edmund, King and Martyr, in their town called Kingsbrig."

Stones from this original chapel were incorporated in the 15th century reconstruction of the building, which also retains the original font. When Bishop Stafford of Exeter consecrated the church in 1414, the Buckfast Abbot also secured the right to bury parishioners in and around the building.

One burial more than three centuries later was recorded with an epitaph on a gravestone now set and highlighted in the south east corner of the church exterior.

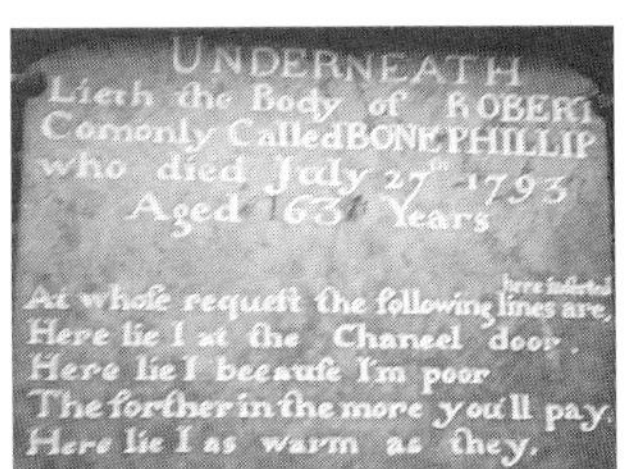

These words are quoted around the English-speaking world: "Underneath lieth the body of Robert, commonly called Bone Phillip, who died July 27th, 1793, aged 63 years. At whose request the following lines are here inserted:

Here lie I at the chancel door,
Here lie I because I'm poor,
The farther in the more you'll pay –
Here lie I as warm as they."

Inside, a wall memorial with a Latin inscription, written by a son-in-law, extols the virtues of George Hughes, who was ejected as Vicar of St Andrew's, Plymouth, in 1662 because of his staunch Protestant views. After imprisonment on Drake's Island in Plymouth Sound, he retired to Kingsbridge, where he was buried at the age of 64 after "doing the best things and suffering the worst".

An artistic gem was provided by John Flaxman (1755–1826), noted for his statues in Westminster Abbey and St Paul's Cathedral. The mother and child delicately depicted by the sculptor were Frances Hawkins, wife of Captain John Hawkins, and her infant daughter, who both died during a sea voyage from Bombay to England in 1817.

The occasion when troops stationed at Kingsbridge sailed off to serve King George III in the American War of Independence is recorded in a local ballad, which ends:

Now God preserve our Monarch, I will finish up my strain;
Be his subjects ever loyal, and his honour all maintain.
May the Lord our voyage prosper, and our arms across the sea,
And put down the wicked rebels in North America.

Perhaps the last landmark they saw as they sailed over the horizon was the spire of St Edmund's.

ALL SAINTS CHURCH, WEST ALVINGTON

ALVINTONA, as it was known in the Domesday records, had status as a Royal manor in Saxon days, when it is thought that a "minster", that is to say a large church served by a cell of monks, was established and sustained by the Royal purse.

On this site, where people have worshipped for at least 1100 years, the 15th century Church of All Saints, its lofty tower topped with four crocketed pinnacles, overlooks Kingsbridge, and affords panoramic views of coast and countryside.

In King John's reign (1199–1216) the revenues of this Royal estate were passed to "Old Sarum", and the Dean and Chapter of Salisbury have retained the right to appoint the clergy here, jointly with the Bishop of Exeter, to this day.

Most of the present building was constructed in local materials, but the high arcades were made of Beer stone, which was shipped around the coast.

The oldest memorial is a high canopied tomb and Easter sepulchre situated on the north side of the chancel, with three brass shields.

An ancient authority claimed that the tomb commemorated "one Bowring, owner of Bowringsleigh" – and his restored home retains a private chapel with a fine coloured screen rescued from the ruins of nearby South Huish Church in 1869.

West Alvington parish originally covered the area of Malborough, Salcombe, South Huish, and South Milton, which all originated as chapels of All Saints.

The present screen is a good example of modern carving and incorporates parts of the mediaeval screen which was dismantled when the church was restored by the Rev Dr Alfred Earle in 1867 when he was Vicar.

Author Sabine Baring-Gould, Rector of Lewtrenchard, described "the destruction" of the old screen as "crass" and wrote: "Clergy should be guardians, not the ravagers, of their churches." It is recorded that when the screen was taken down, a human bone was discovered – probably a saint's relic hidden at the time of the Reformation – and discreetly incorporated in the wood of the new section.

Later Dr Earle became Bishop of Malborough in West London (see note on Malborough Church), and subsequently Dean of Exeter.

Entering the church from the south porch, the visitor is welcomed by a figure of St Hugh of Lincoln set in a niche over the door. A notice explains that it is "in loving memory" of Hugh Copeland Baron Lethbridge, Vicar from 1930 to 1945.

St Hugh (c1135–1200), a Christian in the best sense of the word in his less enlightened times, was praised by John Ruskin as "the most beautiful sacerdotal figure known to me in history".

ALL SAINTS CHURCH, MALBOROUGH

"CATHEDRAL of the South Hams" is the title given in the guide book to All Saints, Malborough. Conspicuous for many miles around, the imposing outline of the church and its spire gives visual support to this claim. The prominent hilltop where it stands also served as a bonfire beacon point to warn of the Armada's progress up the Channel in 1588.

That first impression given to approaching travellers of an imposing church building is confirmed on entering the high, light, and spacious nave through the fine south porch.

Although it was originally established as a chapel of its neighbouring parish of West Alvington, the age of the church is confirmed on entry by the impressive sight of the square arcaded font set on a solid central shaft with four corner supports.

Like West Alvington, from the 12th century the church came under the care of Salisbury Cathedral, and their bishop's register confirms that, before the Reformation, Malborough had a special connection of its own because of the "Paghille Prebend" income from the parish, which helped to endow the Wiltshire Cathedral with an even greater spire.

Arches of the favoured Beer stone enhance the beauty of the nave, which was reconstructed in the 15th century.

Thomas Pyle was Vicar of Malborough for 66 years until his death in 1808 – truly the service of a lifetime.

Tablets on a north wall are in memory of three members of the De Courcy family, the Lords Kinsale, premier Barons of Ireland, whose home in Salcombe (then part of Malborough parish) is now the Marine Hotel. It is claimed that the 30th baron used to upset Queen Victoria by exercising an hereditary claim to keep his hat on in the presence of the Sovereign.

A connection with another 19th century celebrity is the side altar designed by R. H. Froude as a replica of the high altar in Cologne Cathedral. One of the three famous sons of Albert Froude, the Rector of Dartington and Archdeacon of Totnes, he was a leader with Newman and Keble of the Oxford (High Church) Tractarian movement. His brother, J. A. Froude, the historian, is buried at Salcombe.

Two undamaged sections of the mediaeval screen were saved when the Rev Dr Alfred Earle arranged for the extensive Victorian restoration of the building. He became Archdeacon of Totnes and later followed his friend, Bishop Frederick Temple, from Exeter to London Diocese. When Temple appointed him as Suffragan Bishop of West London, Earle took the title of Bishop of Malborough, reflecting the fond association he had with this parish. The bishop's choice may be taken as further proof that this fine building indeed deserves the title, Cathedral of the South Hams.

HOLY TRINITY CHURCH, SALCOMBE

WITH spectacular views of Salcombe's estuary and its steep protecting hills, Holy Trinity Church has a favoured position in one of Devon's best loved resorts.

Earliest mention of Christian worship in Salcombe was at a private chapel at "Ilton Castle". In 1401 Bishop Stafford of Exeter gave licence for divine service in a chapel "constructed anew", but a record of 1755 reported that the building was in ruins. It was rebuilt in 1801.

The present church was provided by the Earl of Devon, Lord of the Manor. A wall inscription reads: "This church was built in the year 1843 and has been made capable of accommodating 563 persons. Andrew Pinwill and William Fletcher, Churchwardens." The Pinwill family influence is apparent in many Devon churches through the beautiful carving by Miss Violet Pinwill (see St Peter and St Paul, Ermington). A good sample of her talent is to be seen here in the pulpit, which depicts figures of the Apostles.

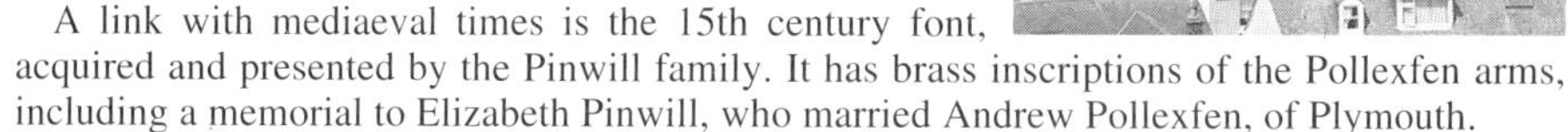

A link with mediaeval times is the 15th century font, acquired and presented by the Pinwill family. It has brass inscriptions of the Pollexfen arms, including a memorial to Elizabeth Pinwill, who married Andrew Pollexfen, of Plymouth.

J. A. Froude, an historian whose books had a flow of language resembling Macaulay, ended his days here and was buried in the churchyard in 1894. He was one of the three gifted sons of the Vicar of Dartington (see All Saints, Malborough).

The Second World War was a time of upheaval in the town, which was "invaded" by no less than a thousand East End children, who were billeted in residents' homes.

The greatest impact, however, was the takeover by the Americans, who assembled vessels and troops here in preparation for the Normandy invasion. It is therefore no surprise to find the Stars and Stripes hanging from the south wall alongside a memorial tablet. It reads: "In memory of those servicemen of the United States of America for whom this place was a true home and who gave their lives for freedom 1943–1945." The flag was presented by Captain D. James Knorr, United States Navy, on behalf of the United States Ambassador and dedicated by Chaplain Lt Mark Farris USN on 21 July 1990.

A frequent visitor was the Poet Laureate, Alfred Lord Tennyson. He was in a yacht anchored in Salcombe estuary on an evening in 1889 when he wrote one of his masterpieces, "Crossing the Bar";

Sunset and evening star,
And one clear call for me!
And may there be no moaning of the bar,
When I put out to sea,

But such a tide as moving seems asleep,
Too full for sound and foam,
When that which drew from out the boundless deep
Turns again home.

Twilight and evening bell,
And after that the dark!
And may there be no sadness of farewell,
When I embark;

For tho' from out our bourne of Time and Place
The flood may bear me far,
I hope to see my Pilot face to face
When I have crosst the bar.

Tennyson died three years later, in 1892.

ST NICHOLAS AND ST CYRIAC CHURCH, SOUTH POOL

BUILT of slate quarried locally, perhaps in the neighbouring parish of Charleton, the Church of St Nicholas and St Cyriac has a fascinating history which is covered in detail in two excellent guides available in the bookstall.

The building stands on a steep hill above its village, by general consent one of the loveliest in Devon, at the head of a valley created by one of the streams running into the Kingsbridge Estuary.

The manor granted at the Conquest to Judhael of Totnes appears to have been acquired soon after by the De La Pole family – perhaps the name South "Pool" was derived from one of them – who may well have been responsible for building the first Norman church. The elegant red sandstone font has survived from those times. The fine 15th century screen, with sections carefully restored, also draws favourable comment from experts.

The unusual dedication to St Nicholas (Santa Claus) of Asia Minor and St Cyriac, a Bethlehem monk, may be attributed to a William De La Pole, who took part in the Third Crusade to the Holy Land with Richard the Lionheart around 1190.

There are many interesting memorials. One of the earliest is the figure in the south transept identified as Lady Muriel, daughter of Sir Thomas Courtenay (then Lord of the Manor), who married John Dynham. There is a record that Edward III in 1380 presented the Rectory to John Dynham, son and heir of Muriel, daughter and heiress of Thomas Courtenay.

The robed figure of Thomas Bryant, Rector of South Pool, 1501–1541, is to be seen in the chancel where there is an Easter sepulchre. It was recorded that his effigy was "loose and could be moved when the sepulchre was required for Easter ceremonies."

Perhaps most interesting of all are the monuments of the Darre family. One shows Leonard and Joan Darre at prayer with their two sons and three daughters. Joan was the daughter of Sir George Bond, knight, "alderman of London and late mayor of ye said cittye" in the memorable year of 1588. The wealthy trading family gave their name to London's famous Bond Street.

The church guide records the story (too amazing not to be true) of the Rev William Streat, the Rector, who was killed while riding on 11 June 1666. While his fiancée, Miss Dorothy Ford, grieved deeply, friends of the couple saw the late young Rector's image in dreams, protesting that he could not rest until he had fulfilled his promise to marry. His body was exhumed on 27 November 1666, and standing beside him before the altar, the bride made her vows. He was immediately reburied, and there were no further apparitions. It seems everybody lived and died happily ever after. A bit macabre, maybe, but a romantic tale in a beautiful setting.

ST WINWALLOE'S CHURCH, EAST PORTLEMOUTH

FROM the steep hill rising up to St Winwalloe's Church, East Portlemouth, by general consent the views of the estuary below take one's breath away.

The dedication to St Winwalloe, the only one in England, has raised speculation that a church has occupied this site since the time when Celtic missionaries set up cells of monks and monasteries in Cornwall and Devon. Winwalloe's story may be vague, but that only adds to its romantic quality. It would seem that with his family he fled from Wales to Normandy in the wake of the first Saxon invasions. When the Celtic missionaries returned from their new base at Landevennec Monastery, Finisterre, was Winwalloe among them? Sabine Baring-Gould believed that it was not improbable, because Winwalloe was closely related to the reigning princes of the region, including Cado, Duke of Cornwall, who was a cousin. The link between the church and the monastery was cemented in 1985, when the Finisterre Abbot sent a scroll of greeting to commemorate the 1500th anniversary of the saint's birth.

Whatever buildings were here earlier, the present mainly 15th century structure was probably sponsored by prosperous local shipbuilders who had provided vessels for the French wars in the 14th century and would send one or more ships to pursue the Armada in 1588.

The ancient screen, saved by Rector John Cleland when he hid it from the destructive Roundheads during the Civil War, has some remarkable figure paintings, including one of St Winwalloe holding a church in his hand.

An official report of 1553 reveals that Edward VI's officer, the Earl of Bedford, ordered that a silver cross in the church should be sold to finance essential works to strengthen the harbour "for the defence of the country". Parishioners were further required to refund the value of the cross to the Church Goods Commissioners.

A sad story is told on the tombstone of Richard Jarvis, who died on 25 May 1782, aged 79. "Through poison he was cut off and brought to death at last. It was by his apprentice girl on whom there's sentence passed. Oh may all people warning take, for she was burned at the stake." One source claims that the girl, Rebecca Dowing, was the last person to be burned for witchcraft in England. Her execution took place at Ringwell, Exeter.

East Portlemouth rivals East Budleigh and Salcombe Regis in East Devon with tales of piracy and smuggling – and in the practice of raiding coastal wrecks. There is an oft-repeated and embellished story of a Rector of East Portlemouth who was preaching to a snoozy congregation at matins one Sunday morning when the clerk came and whispered in his ear. Off came the rector's gown, and he woke the parishioners as he descended from the pulpit with a cry; "There's a wreck at Prawle Point. Let's all start fair!"

Whatever their reasons, two men were glad to occupy that pulpit in the course of 100 years – John Rumbelow began his ministry in 1691, and his successor John Grantham preached his last sermon after 60 years as rector in 1791.

The church has an active Friends Association, and there is a screen with photos of the many parish activities, as well as legends of St Winwalloe. A special magazine was published, with a series of wide-ranging articles from parishioners, to celebrate the arrival of the year AD 2000.

ST SYLVESTER'S CHURCH, CHIVELSTONE

THERE is a typical South Hams view from St Sylvester's, Chivelstone, down the long valley to the gleaming estuary below.

The church's dedication to a 4th century Pope – unique for England – gives rise to speculation. Sylvester became Pope in 314, soon after Constantine was acknowledged as the Roman Emperor and stopped all persecution of Christians throughout the empire. It may be significant that Sylvester's mother was a British princess, whose family may have been known to Constantine while he was stationed in Britain. One tradition claims that Sylvester baptised Constantine, who was the first Roman emperor openly to profess Christianity.

A Domesday estate, after the Conquest Chivelstone became the property of Judhael of Totnes. It appears that when a chapel was first built here it was served by priests from the church at Stokenham.

Another chapel was established in Chivelstone parish at Prawle Point (meaning "look-out hill"), the most southerly headland in Devon. Its dedication to St Brendan (c486–c578), an Irish missionary famous for his travels, was also unique. The Prawle chapel, however, has long since disappeared.

As a venue for peaceful meditation, St Sylvester's cannot be bettered. Its greatest treasure, the 15th century pulpit, elaborately carved (except for the hinged door) out of a single bole of oak, is a work of art to be seen and never forgotten. It is believed to have been hewn by Thomas Prideaux of Ashburton, and one enthusiastic architectural expert, J. M. Slader in his *Churches of Devon,* gives a detailed appraisal of the carving, writing that it has "a freedom and vigour rarely found in Perpendicular work."

The other outstanding feature of the church's interior is the screen made from Spanish chestnut, also in the 15th century, with pictures of apostles and bishops, including St Sylvester, painted in gold, red, and green. The work was restored with typical skill by Herbert Read of Exeter in 1979. One of figures on the screen has been identified as the little-known 6th century monk St Placid, a name that surely matches the atmosphere which pervades this remote southernmost parish in the Diocese of Exeter.

ST WERBERGH'S CHURCH, WEMBURY

SECURELY set on its headland by Wembury Bay, St Werbergh's Church has been a landmark for sailors over the centuries. The views from its high vantage point, to the west along the coast to the entrance of Plymouth Sound and southward over the Channel, are breathtaking.

Belief that Christians have worshipped on this site for 1200 years or more finds expression in the stained glass picture of St Werbergh holding a Saxon Church in her hand at the west end of the present building.

The rare dedication (there is another in Cornwall) is explained by an ancient source: "Christian Saxons erected a small oratory here to St Werbergh, daughter of the pagan Wulfhere, King of Mercia, and niece of St Etheldreda. St Werbergh was an abbess, whose shrine at Chester attracted pilgrims until the Reformation."

Another source describes Wembury as one of the oldest Devon churches which came under the first Plympton minster or priory in the reign of King Edgar (959 – 975). Plympton priors (for an annual income of £50) later became responsible for arranging services at what they regarded as a distant outpost in mediaeval times.

The 1535 Exeter Bishop's Register reported that priests travelling from Plympton were "in great jeopardy of life" in rain, hail and snow. Three had died in the course of duty. Further, the prior was not willing to send a priest to bury anyone for less than 7d (3p).

There are several fine memorials to local families who took over the care of the church after the dissolution of the priory. Most striking is the large Jacobean limestone monument to Sir John Hele, his wife and children, of Wembury Manor.

The sixth son of a younger brother, Sir John made his fortune, first as Recorder at Exeter, and finally as Sergeant at Law for James I, in which role he took part in the trial of Sir Walter Raleigh in 1603.

Another lawyer, Vincent Calmady, in 1555 bought the Domesday manor of Langdon. The most conspicuous memorial of this family, who lived in the parish for 300 years, is one in Italian marble in memory of Elizabeth, daughter of Josias Calmady and wife of Sir John Narborough, a 17th century admiral. The font now used was the gift of an Admiral Calmady, of Langdon, in 1820.

Another parishioner, Major Edmund Lockyer, won fame on 21 January 1837, when he hoisted the Union Flag to claim Western Australia for the Crown. Commemorative flags presented by the State Government hang in the south aisle, and there is a framed picture of St Werbergh's Church, Mt Barker, West Australia.

This place steeped in historical mementoes also has a literary connection with John Galsworthy, author of the *Forsyte Saga* novels, whose family had links with the parish. As the series ends, Soames Forsyte, the leading character, writes these verses about the church when he visits his ancestral home at Wembury:

Here stand I buttressed over the sea!
Time and sky take no toll from me.
Shall I fall, leaving my flock of graves?
Not for all your rebelling waves!
I stand fast; let the waters cry,
Here I last to Eternity.

ST BARTHOLOMEW'S CHURCH, YEALMPTON

PREHISTORIC caves once inhabited by extinct animals, an ancient gravestone to Goreus or Toreus (perhaps a Roman-British chieftain), church memorials to two of Devon's three oldest families, and the original cottage where Old Mother Hubbard lived – Yealmpton parish has provided enough material to occupy the most ardent antiquarians, amateur or professional.

Tristram Risdon, writing his survey of the County of Devon between 1600 and 1630, claimed that "Ethelbald [King of Wessex 855–860] according to tradition, had his palace here."

There is evidence that a cell of priests set up a "minster" in Saxon times to serve parishioners both in and around the settlement, which had one of the 120 churches existing at the time of the Devon Domesday survey of Osbern, Bishop of Exeter (1072 – 1103).

With such historic parish links, the visitor may be surprised to be confronted with a comparatively modern church. The design is in fact an example of the work of one of England's most famous Victorian architects, William Butterfield. Described by Poet Laureate John Betjeman as "the most amazing building of its kind", the interior is enriched by the use of variegated local marbles.

Memorials from the early church which have been preserved in the new structure include the names Crocker and Coplestone, a reminder of the verse often quoted (and sometimes disputed) by Devonians: "Crocker, Cruwys, and Coplestone, when the Conqueror came were all at home." Sir John Crocker, of Lyneham, who had two wives both called Alicia, served at Agincourt. There is a brass memorial to his son (died 1508), who was standard bearer to Edward IV.

Experts delight in discussing the brass memorial of Isabel Coplestone, which is a palimpest, that is to say an inscription carved on the reverse side of an earlier memorial to James, possibly a 15th century Flemish cleric. There is speculation as to how the brass came to Yealmpton.

Monuments in the south aisle to the Bastard family, of Kitley, who attained the property through marriage to the Pollexfens, include the names of Edmund and Colonel John Bastard, who saved the Plymouth docks from being destroyed in a riot in 1799. A memorial pays tribute to the short life of Edmund Pollexfen Bastard, who "restored and beautified" the church in 1851, aged 31 years.

The original version of the song "Old Mother Hubbard" was composed, it is said, in 1805 by Sarah Martin, who visited her sister, the wife of Squire Bastard, of Kitley House. Sarah retired, a disappointed spinster, to the now famous thatched cottage, which latterly has been in use as a restaurant.

When the church tower collapsed in 1911, the Vicar made an appeal, using the pen name "Old Mother Hubbard", pointing out that without public support, the church cupboard was bare. The Press seized upon the story, and gifts came from across the nation to enable the tower to be rebuilt in 1915.

HOLY CROSS CHURCH, NEWTON FERRERS

LIKE twin sentinels, Holy Cross, Newton Ferrers, and St Peter's, Revelstoke, stand overlooking the inlet reaching back from Wembury Bay to greet the River Yealm at the end of its journey from Dartmoor.

The fine modern gate at the higher entrance to Holy Cross Church, with the date AD2000 and the welcoming text: "I am the way...", tells the visitor that there is a continuing devotion for this place where Christians have congregated for more than 1000 years.

The first wooden Saxon church, recorded by Bishop Osbern c1080, was replaced by a Norman building of stone, probably provided by the feudal de Ferrers family, who counted this among the many English manors they received from William the Conqueror. Links have recently been revived with their Normandy home, Ferriere St Hilaire. The first named rector in 1279 was Herbert de Ferrariis, a member of the family. One source claims that he was presented to the living by an Isolda de Ferrers, who may have been his mother.

The building, which has seen many changes over the centuries, is restful and interesting, with many signs of being a centre of spiritual life in the present. Aline Stackhouse's excellent 1998 guide gives a full description of church life from the earliest to the most recent times. The outline structure of the building is mainly 15th century, with a 13th century chancel.

Listed among the rectors, William Bradbridge (1572–1578) was in fact the Bishop of Exeter. After the Reformation the Bishops of Exeter Diocese, previously one of the best endowed in the nation, were forced to seek extra income. Queen Elizabeth permitted Bradbridge to receive the tithes from Newton Ferrers and other parishes. He did, however, spend time in the parish and hold ordinations in the church, and he died and was buried here, although his final resting place was Exeter Cathedral.

For 300 years the Yonges of Puslinch have taken a leading role in church activities. No less than eight members of the family have been Rectors, the most remarkable service being given by the Rev John Yonge, who held office for 65 years from 1812 to 1877. The east window was erected in his memory when the church was restored in 1886.

The granite and alabaster font was given in 1885 by Miss Charlotte M. Yonge, the famous novelist, and Miss Mary Yonge. Charlotte also wrote in 1873 a biography of John Coleridge Patteson, who left his Alfington parish at Ottery St Mary to become a missionary in the South Seas and first Bishop of Melanesia. Martyred in 1871, one of his Devon memorials is the Exeter Cathedral pulpit.

The charming Yealm Tapestry on display in the church, completed in 1990 after 3000 hours' work by a group of volunteers, includes the twin Churches of Newton Ferrers and Revelstoke.

Returning through the churchyard, which contains the tombstone of Waterloo veteran Field Marshal Lord Seaton and Elizabeth his wife (daughter of the Rev James Yonge), we come again to the AD2000 Millennium Gate, and gladly accept its scriptural blessing, "Go in peace," as we go on our way.

ST PETER'S CHURCH, REVELSTOKE & ST PETER'S, NOSS MAYO

LORD Revelstoke's Victorian Church of St Peter, from its perch carved into the south hill, looks across the creek to Holy Cross, Newton Ferrers. One of England's most prominent men in his day, Lord Revelstoke (formerly Mr E. C. Baring of the famous banking family) took his title from this parish in 1885, having acquired the Domesday Membland property in 1877.

Here he entertained (among others) the Prince of Wales (later Edward VII), Prime Minister Gladstone, the Russian Czar, and Baron Rothschild, and on fine days took them along "The Nine-Mile Drive" which he had constructed. It is still enjoyed as a wide grassy coastal footway by walkers.

The family name, Revel's Stoke, is derived from Richard de Rivell, Sheriff of Devon 1198–1199, who was lord of the manor of Stoke on the western shores of Bigbury Bay. With the sea lapping or roaring, the original Church of St Peter was built into the low cliffside, one and a half miles from the present St Peter's. One of the 120 Devon Churches mentioned in Bishop Osbern's survey of 1073, like St Werbergh's, Wembury, it served as a landmark for ships making their way to and from Plymouth Sound.

Although it was an impressive place of worship, Noss Mayo villagers found it a long trek, particularly during inclement winter weather, and were allowed by Bishop Stafford (1395–1419) to hold services in a chapel (now lost) probably at the head of the Noss Mayo creek.

A storm in 1868 wrought such havoc on the exposed building that it was finally abandoned as a place of worship; but its ruins remain a shrine, retaining the haunted air of its romantic past, commanding maritime views that continue to reward pilgrims who come this way.

Consecrated in 1882 by Bishop Frederick Temple (later Bishop of London and eventually Archbishop of Canterbury), the new church constructed of Devon granite and marble was finally completed in 1888 at a cost of £34,000 – a fortune in those days.

As the main contributor, Lord Revelstoke spared no expense, employing a famous London architect, Mr Piers St Aubyn, for the overall design. For most of the interior furnishing he made a point of using the considerable talents of Devon craftsmen, in particular the wood carver Harry Hems of Exeter, who included in his bench-end designs an old sea battle, recalling the part played by members of the Baring family in Elizabethan days. Another bench-end records: "Harry Hems and his Merry Men carved all these bench ends at Exeter AD1882." The pulpit, with scenes from the lives of St Paul and St Stephen, is another artistic gem.

The church notes record that Edward VII so liked the church organ made by Walker and Sons of London that he had a facsimile installed in his Sandringham Parish Church.

In 1982, celebrating the church's centenary, the main roof was renewed, the tower repointed, and the tower clock's face restored to its pristine gilded beauty – thanks to local initiative and help from English Heritage.

ALL SAINTS CHURCH, HOLBETON

PRAISE for the craftsmanship in All Saints, Holbeton, as being "treasured in a village church and worthy of a great cathedral" is quoted from Arthur Mee's *Book of Devon* in the church's detailed guidebook by P. G. Heppenstall. With so much to see, only the visitor with many hours to spare can absorb every detail.

There are two fonts – one of Devon marble was installed at the church's restoration in 1885, the other of Norman origin (about 1160) is a reminder that this has been a centre of worship for many centuries.

Holbeton parish, which includes a section of the spectacular coastline, had four Saxon estates mentioned in Domesday records, including Flete and Membland.

Originally Polsloe Priory in Exeter was endowed with income from the parish along with the advowson (the right to appoint clergy). This has reverted to the Crown.

An early Norman building was extended in the 13th century, and Bishop Grandisson dedicated the high altar in 1336.

The 120-foot spire was raised in the 15th century.

The Hele family monument, added in the 17th century, includes figures of Thomas Hele of Exeter, Sheriff of Devon 1600–1601; his son, Thomas Hele of Flete; and the latter's wife, a Champernowne of Modbury. Their son, Sir Thomas Hele, made a baronet by Charles I in 1627, was also Sheriff of Devon and MP for Okehampton.

Another family is remembered in the Lady Chapel window with the dedication: "Many generations lie buried here of the Hillersdons, once of Membland, whose chapel this was. They intermarried with amongst other families in the county, those of Edgcombe, Fortescue, Kirkham, Courtenay, Copleston, Chudleigh, Champernowne, Harris, Hele, Crocker, and Frind."

The east window text reads: "John Crocker Bulteel, High Sheriff of Devon 1841, married in 1826 Lady Elizabeth Grey, second daughter of Charles, second Lord Grey, to whose memory this window was erected."

Henry Bingham Mildmay, father of the first Lord Mildmay, carried out a major restoration of the church in 1885, which included carving of a quality praised by J. M. Slader in his *Churches of Devon*: "The skill of some modern carvers is equal to that of their mediaeval predecessors."

The eye is drawn to the modern stained glass window commemorating the First and Second Lords Mildmay, of Flete (died 1947 and 1950), and J. C. Bulteel (1956), his wife and daughter.

Full of historic interest, the Holbeton Parish Map Tapestry was started in 1994, and by the time it was completed in 1998 seventy parishioners had played a part in making it. A 30-page guide explains the 23 sections in detail, each portraying outstanding natural features and buildings in the parish.

Connected by marriage and by their joint stock-market activities, the Bulteel and Baring (Lord Revelstoke) families in 1889 built a lodge at the boundaries of their two estates, Flete and Membland, with their emblems, the Bull and the Bear (note the pun on their names) on the gate pillars. Do the "bull" and "bear" terms used in stock exchange variations really derive from this?

The tapestry was finally completed in another featured landmark, the Reading Room, which was originally built in the 19th century as a school by benefactor Mr John Scott, churchwarden and Plymouth brewer, the father of Robert Falcon Scott of Antarctic fame.

ALL SAINTS CHURCH, THURLESTONE

STANDING in an immaculate churchyard, on a promontory in sight and sound of the sea, All Saints Church, Thurlestone, once carried a fire beacon on its tower as a lighthouse for shipping. It was used, folklore says, when the English fleet engaged with the Spanish Armada. Named after the "rock with a hole" – the long-standing natural feature out in the bay (first mentioned in a Saxon charter of 845) – Thurlestone has not had to strive to win its reputation as one of Devon's favourite resorts.

It is thought that an original church here was replaced by the de Ferrers family with the present structure of local stone in the 13th century, and records reveal that Sir Hugh de Ferrers, an underlord of the Baron of Totnes, appointed his kinsman, Ralph de Ferrers, as Rector in 1280.

Once again we find that the most treasured item inside is the handsome 12th century font, made of red Devon sandstone with a honeysuckle design. Well protected now because of thefts in 1994–95 of ancient carvings and a bishop's chair is a Prayer Book published in the reign of Charles I, which must have been even more securely hidden in the time of Oliver Cromwell, who ordered all such books to be destroyed.

John Snell, the rector of those times, who was also a chaplain of Charles I, was forced to flee (perhaps with the Prayer Book under his arm) after the surrender of Salcombe Castle to the Parliamentarian troops. Somehow he managed to survive until the Restoration of Charles II to the throne in 1660, and was reinstated in his Rectory. Mr Snell was also a Canon of Exeter Cathedral. His son George succeeded him as rector and became Archdeacon of Totnes.

An architectural gem, the 16th century porch has a boss picturing Elizabeth of York, whose marriage to Henry VII, of Lancaster marked the end of the Wars of the Roses. Local legend tells of goods smuggled from France being stored above this porch, with the well-rewarded connivance of certain rectors, until early in the 19th century.

Thomas Stephens, who died during Cromwell's Commonwealth in 1658, is commemorated in a Lady Chapel wall monument, kneeling and attended by three sons, opposite his wife with their four daughters. Rector Henry Luscombe (died 1634) is also here portrayed at prayer.

Recognition of one rector's powerful influence in church and community life from 1839 to 1895 is found in the inscription: "To Peregrine Arthur Ilbert, who for 55 years lived among and for his parishioners, this tablet and the east window were erected by some of those who loved him. 1904." There is also a memorial window (designed by Captain Robert Falcon Scott's widow) to his son, Sir Courtenay Ilbert, who was Clerk of the House of Commons.

Another tablet records that the Royal Marines, who had an officer cadet school in the nearby Thurlestone Hotel during the Second World War, worshipped in the church. Reunions were held in 1995 and 1997, and silver candlesticks presented by members of the wartime school are in regular use.

ALL SAINTS CHURCH, SOUTH MILTON

WITH its village and 12th century Church in a combe leading down to the sea by spectacular Thurlestone Rock, which is "in the parish", South Milton plays its unique part in the charm of Devon's South Hams. Settled with its centre of worship from at least Saxon times, the village was recorded as "Milteltona" in the Domesday record. Like Malborough and South Huish, All Saints Church came under the ecclesiastical care of West Alvington from the early days, with which a lasting link is the Norman font of most unusual design.

Who or what do the carved figures represent? Is this a dancer, perhaps Salome? Is this the face of John the Baptist? Experts have their own ideas. J. M. Slader says: "The decoration incorporates cable and zig-zag mouldings, depicting two animals and a woman falling backwards – the meaning is not clear." Arthur Mee saw "the head of a demon and other crude figures." *South Milton, the Story of a Village* declares: "The font is by far the most curious and fascinating in the district." Discussing the images, it conjectures they may represent Adam and Eve, the Norman lord of South Milton and his lady; the head with pointed ears might be "a devil, a Dane, or a Satyr." Clearly this item deserves a second look!

Bishop Bronescombe blessed the building in 1269, and the first vicar named after records became obligatory was Sir Thomas de Kentisbury, instituted in 1309. Names associated with the church and manor include Sir William Peppard, the Carews of Haccombe, the Rupe or Roope family, Walter Prideaux (attorney of Totnes), and the Ilbert family (see also Thurlestone).

An old slab has been observed with the inscription: "Matthew Roope of Whitlocksworthy, within this psh, gent, died 15th October, 1598. Joan his wife, daughter of Adam Strode of Innaton."

Another feature which has also drawn praise from experts is the 15th century screen. Bligh Bond observes: "A beautiful screen of Perpendicular character with figures of saints." Prof. W. G. Hoskins also comments on the beauty of the carving and figure paintings, which saw the light of day again when brown varnish was removed. When and why the varnish was applied remains a mystery.

It is thought that one of the fields south of the church, called The Vineyard, once grew vines to provide wine both for use at communion and for the comfort of the clergy.

The parish was finally granted its independence from West Alvington in 1886 and has since been linked to form a single benefice with its neighbour, Thurlestone.

ST LAWRENCE CHURCH, BIGBURY

BURGH Island, linked at low tide to the mainland like St Michael's Mount in Cornwall, once also had a chapel dedicated to St Michael on its summit. That building has long since disappeared, but the Church of St Lawrence, set securely inland from the bay, was probably founded by the Bigbury family, who lived in the manor in the 13th century.

Before the Norman Conquest there is a record that the area known as Bichberia was owned by Ordulph, "friend and councillor of Canute and Edward the Confessor". Later the Conqueror's half-brother, Robert Count of Mortain, received the manorial rights.

Taking his name from Burgh Island, it was Sir William de Bigbury who presented Philip Harwedetone to the Rectory of St Lawrence Church in 1274. He was succeeded as rector by Ralph de Bigbury, a member of the family, which remained in the parish until the 15th century. Their name is engraved on the two brasses in memory of William de Bigbury's wife, Joan, and their daughter, Elizabeth. One source claims that a William de Bigbury was killed in a duel, but not before he had appointed a kinsman, John de Bigbury, as Rector of the church in 1414.

The 14th century font had carved upon it the Cross of St George, proof perhaps of the family's loyalty to the Crown. Memorial figures in Elizabethan dress of John Pierce (died 1612) and his wife Jane (1589) have the punning caption (composed by John himself?) "Pierce, being pierced by death, doth peace obtain."

There is a fascinating story surrounding two essential items of church furniture. Bishop Hugh Oldham of Exeter (1504–1519) gave St Andrew's Church, Ashburton, a pulpit and lectern (with his emblem – an owl) carved by a local craftsman in 1510. When Ashburton's curate, the Rev Charles Powlett, was appointed to the living at Bigbury in 1776, he brought with him both the pulpit and the lectern, for which Ashburton Church was paid 11 guineas. Apparently Mr Powlett's new parishioners preferred to have a traditional image on their lectern, so the owl's head was replaced with an eagle – on the owl's body!

ALL HALLOWS CHURCH, RINGMORE

FULL of historical interest, particularly in the lives of two dynamic rectors, All Hallows Church, Ringmore, adorns a remote and beautiful area by the Devon coastline. William Lane, Rector at the time of the Civil War and a keen supporter of King Charles I, mustered a band of parishioners and prepared them for combat. Acquiring some cannon, he and his men trained them onto the bridge over the River Avon in the parish of Aveton Gifford (where he was also rector) and fired on the Roundhead Army as it was passing through to take part in the siege of Salcombe Castle.

As the Parliamentarians gained the ascendancy, they selected Mr Lane as a target for revenge. A band of their troops was despatched from their Plymouth garrison to capture and hang or shoot the belligerent Rector, who swiftly took refuge in a small room with a fireplace tucked away under the tower of Ringmore Church. Here he stayed for three months, being secretly fed by his parishioners, while the Roundheads vainly searched his Rectory and the surrounding countryside. The discomfort was considerable, but Mr Lane's worst moments came on Sundays when he overheard an intruding Cromwellian minister preaching rank heresy from his pulpit. He could scarcely contain his fury.

After escaping to France, Mr Lane returned and vigorously pursued his claims with the mellowing Cromwellian regime to be reinstated, but when it seemed he was at last about to receive compensation, he died from drinking contaminated water in Exeter and was buried in the churchyard of St Michael's, Alphington.

The other remarkable incumbent belonged to the Victorian era. Rector for 52 years, he renovated the church and his memorial for this jubilee of service is the restored chancel. In 1859, soon after the Rev Francis Charles Hingeston started his long ministry here, fights occurred during two Sunday services, when the sexton attempted to keep order as intruders noisily objected to Anglican doctrine. The Press gave a garbled account of the encounters, and the Rector replied with a lengthy letter of explanation, which concluded: "I did put the man who assaulted our sexton out of the church, as I was bound to do." His ministry continued in peace and devotion, both to his parish and the Diocese of Exeter.

Mr Hingeston married Martha Randolph, daughter of the Rev Herbert Randolph, incumbent of Melrose, Scotland, and changed his name to Hingeston-Randolph.

Devon church historian Beatrix Cresswell was full of praise for his magnificent work at the time in transcribing the Registers of the Bishops of Exeter. She wrote: "He provided inexhaustible materials for diocesan and county history. It was a stupendous work to reveal ancient records, formerly inaccessible or illegible to students of history". He became a prebendary of Exeter Cathedral and was succeeded as Rector, on his death in 1910, by his son, the Rev Herbert Castillon Hingeston-Randolph.

The church remains a charming place of worship. The oldest item is the 1170 square font, and the narrow north aisle chapel lends an air of timeless antiquity.

Perhaps R. C. Sherriff found inspiration here at the heart of the peaceful village while he wrote his masterpiece, *Journey's End*. It is fitting that the village inn, where he wrote it, was renamed to take the title of the play.

ST MICHAEL'S CHURCH, BLACKAWTON

ALTHOUGH a church has occupied this secluded site for a thousand years, there can hardly have been a more historic occasion than the meeting here in 1943 when arrangements were made to evacuate the people and their livestock to provide American troops with a training patch for the Normandy invasion.

THIS STONE COMMEMORATES
THE 50th ANNIVERSARY
OF THE TOTAL EVACUATION OF
BLACKAWTON PARISH IN 1943/4
TO ENABLE THE U.S. FORCES
TO TRAIN FOR THE
D-DAY LANDINGS IN FRANCE
AND OUR GRATITUDE
FOR SACRIFICES MADE.
ERECTED IN 1994 BY SOME OF THOSE
EVACUATED AND OTHER
PARISHIONERS AND FRIENDS.

General Eisenhower made his headquarters at Sheplegh Court, a mansion in the parish, and one of the church's treasures, the rood-screen, which bears the insignia of Henry VIII and his first wife Catherine of Aragon, was dismantled and stored for safety. There is a tradition that the screen was originally transferred here from Greyfriars Church on Plymouth Quay, where Catherine first set foot in England when she came to marry Henry.

A tablet erected 50 years after the war ended places the evacuation on record. Admiral A. J. Cawthra was responsible for the redecoration of the Lady Chapel in the 1980s.

Aveton, the original name for the village, was settled in Saxon times, no doubt with a church at its centre. Domesday records: "The King has a manor called Aveton, which Ansger the hunchback held in the reign of King Edward [the Confessor]."

The church came under the care of Plympton Priory, although there was also a connection with Torre Abbey, founded by William Brewer. Plympton abbots were responsible for providing vicars until the monasteries were dissolved c. 1538.

How did the name Aveton become Blackawton? One suggestion is that "black" may refer to the local building stone, which turns dark in the wet.

A brass memorial to Nicholas (died 1582) and Margaret Forde perhaps has some family connection with a John Ford, who in 1539 was bailiff for Torre Abbey of Blackawton Manor.

An enthusiastic expert described the three sedilia (mediaeval stone seats for priests) in the chancel wall as among the finest examples remaining in Devon.

The oldest item, the circular Norman font, was considered by the knowledgeable Miss K. M. Clarke as "the best example of honeysuckle fonts in the county, and with the exception of Paignton, the largest."

The Jacobean pulpit was once set so high that Frederick Temple, Bishop of Exeter 1869–1885, refused to climb into it.

There are several memorials to the Cholwich family, who for two centuries occupied and renovated the ancient Oldstone estate. Oldstone, a name derived from the pre-Conquest Ulf's Tun (or farm), was destroyed by fire in 1895, and the ruins are said to be haunted.

The great Victorian expert on Devon's church bells, the Rev Thomas Ellacombe of Clyst St George, discovered that "Blackawton had the last of all our native bell founders. William Hambling, an ingenious blacksmith who had seen some work done by itinerant founders in Cornwall, succeeded in casting 12 bells for different churches in the area (including one each at Thurlestone and Stokenham) from 1823 to 1845."

ST SAVIOUR'S CHURCH, DARTMOUTH

VISITING the famous Devon port for the first time a century ago, the Rev Sabine Baring-Gould had this to say: "I cannot think that I have seen any sight lovelier than Dartmouth on an evening in early summer, with Kingswear opposite, the one bathed in soft sweet shadow, the other glittering and golden in the sun's declining rays."

Knights of the Second Crusade set out from the port in 1147, and a further 37 ships left Dartmouth to join Richard I on the Third Crusade in 1190.

St Saviour's began as a harbourside chapel, sanctioned by Edward I in 1285 when he inspected the port as launch-pad for his French campaigns, but because of opposition from Devon church leaders the building was not blessed until half a century later. It saved maritime families the trek to the "mother" Church of St Clement's – a mile away and 400 feet up the steep hillside.

Baring-Gould recorded his delight at the church's "magnificent painted and gilt wooden screen and stone pulpit of the same character".

Prosperity came to the town when trading vessels imported wine from Spain and France. Greatest of the merchants was John Hawley, MP and many times Mayor of Dartmouth, who extended St Saviour's. A celebrated brass memorial shows him with his two wives, Joan (died 1394) and Alice (died 1403). Hawley (who died in 1408) is holding Joan's hand, "leaving little doubt as to which wife he loved best," Baring-Gould claimed! Hawley inspired the character "Shipman" for Chaucer, who visited Dartmouth in 1373, and the merchant's uncanny success was put into verse: "Blow the wind high, blow the wind low, it bloweth good to Hawley's Hoe."

Carved timbers from the captured Armada ship, *Nuestra Señora del Rosario*, can still be seen incorporated in the 'new' gallery (1633).

Although dated 1631, an historic door includes much earlier wrought iron work, with the leonine sign of Edward I, whose link with Dartmouth has already been mentioned.

Humphrey Gilbert and Captain Cook prayed here before sailing to claim respectively Newfoundland and Australia for the Crown.

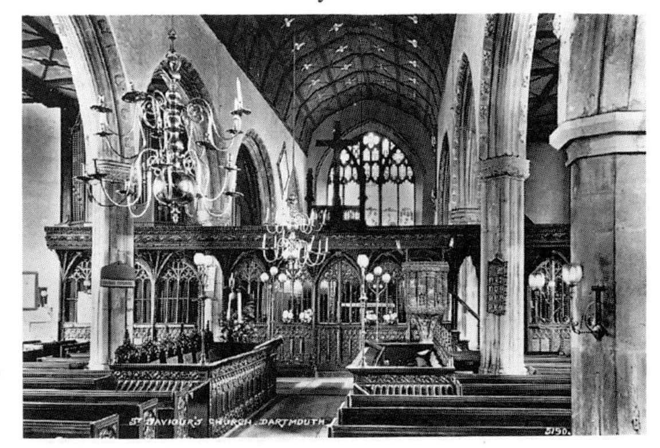

Roundheads occupied the town in 1646, and Puritan John Flavel was Vicar until ejected at the restoration of Charles II. Such was his charisma that Dartmouth people continued to walk six miles on a Sunday to hear him preach at Slapton Church.

Baptised in 1663, Thomas Newcomen was the great-grandson of the rector of nearby Stoke Fleming. His memorial recalls that by experimenting in his Dartmouth laboratory "he was the first to conceive the idea of working pistons by steam" – the system later developed by Watts.

The Holdsworth family's influence on Dartmouth as MPs, Mayors, and Governors of Dartmouth Castle has a memorial in the sedate Corporation pews, carved in 1816, while Robert Holdsworth was Vicar.

ST PETROX CHURCH, DARTMOUTH

EVEN the most careful historical writers find it hard to resist the tradition that St Petrock himself landed at this picturesque spot 1,400 years ago and founded a chapel on the rocky foundation from which his name is derived. An ancient deed of 1192 mentions a "monastery of St Peter" on this site. Served by a small band of monks or priests, this chapel and similar oratories along the coast were landmarks for sailors.

St Petrox (the mediaeval version of St Petrock's) continued to be used for worship under the care of Stoke Fleming Church until it found a new role when the castle was built in the 14th and 15th centuries.

Three brasses from the early 17th century are in memory of John Roope, Barbara Plumleigh, and Dorothy Roys. Members of a branch of the Plumleigh family in the United States maintain a connection with the church. Among my valued possessions is a gift of three fine pictures of Barbara Plumleigh, her four daughters, and her two sons, made many years ago from rubbings of this brass by Mr and Mrs Geoffrey Ghey, of Dartmouth Naval College. Because of the danger of theft, however, the church brasses can now be viewed only by request from the vicar and churchwardens.

It was interesting to read in the Devon Studies Library that these very objects were targets for vandalism even 100 years ago by "trippers who hacked out the brasses with penknives as souvenirs."

There are memorials of the Holdsworth family, who were Governors of the castle for 200 years, and of Dartmouth merchants, the Newmans. A descendant, Sir Robert Newman Bt, moved to Mamhead House on Haldon Moor in 1823 and became MP for Exeter. This manor stayed in the hands of the Newmans until the death in 1945 of Sir Robert Newman, later Baron Mamhead of Exeter. He, too, was MP for Exeter for 13 years and made the mansion's cellars available to store Exeter Cathedral treasures during the Second World War.

The east window in St Petrox was installed in 1927 in memory of George Parker Bidder, the brilliant 19th century mathematician and engineer. Known as the "Calculating Boy", he was born in Okehampton and, after constructing London's Victoria Docks and inventing the swing railway bridge, returned to Devon at last to be buried in Stoke Fleming churchyard.

St Petrox shows every sign of being greatly loved and cared for by those who worship here.

ST MARY'S CHURCH, TOTNES

LEGENDS claim that Brutus, who came from Troy and was the ancestor of Kings Lear, Cymbeline, Cole, and Arthur of Camelot, first landed at Totnes to become father of the British race.

A rough old rock marked "Brutus Stone", now set in the High Street, is said to have been the first object the Trojan stepped on as he landed, and is the point where Totnes Mayors by tradition proclaim each new British monarch.

Regardless of the romantic past, Totnes is fair enough to commend herself, as the view overlooking the River Dart from the 120-foot church tower testifies. How the tower was built is a human tale echoed in many parishes to this day.

The old Norman building was without a tower, so parishioners, determined that only the best would do, visited Tavistock, Callington, and Ashburton to seek inspiration. At last in 1452 the Mayor and Vicar went house-to-house to ask for contributions from the townspeople, only to find that the "offerings came in reluctantly as they are wont to do." Help came from Bishop Lacy of Exeter, who gave 40 days' indulgence from their sins to all who contributed, and the structure which rose is rightly described as "handsome" by W. G. Hoskins in his book on Devon.

Totnes was a prosperous Saxon Borough with a Royal Mint at the time of the Norman Conquest, when William 1 bestowed town and church on Juhel, a Breton.

In 1088, Juhel gave "to God and Tetbald Abbot of Angers the key of the Church of St Mary Totnes and its lands." Historian Beatrix Cresswell imagined the scene of "Saxon burgesses looking on with mixed feelings as the crowd of Normans, Bretons, and French processed into their old church."

Totnes Priory was built as a cell of the abbey, and in the 12th century a leper hospital was founded with a chapel dedicated to Mary Magdalene.

In 1414 a quarrel between the prior and a certain John Southam led to blood being spilled in the church, which was closed pending an inquiry by Bishop Stafford. When the affair was settled, it was resolved to rebuild the Norman church. The screen built by order of the Totnes Corporation 1449–1450 is universally admired as "lace work in Beer stone".

There is a memorial to Mayor Walter Smith (died 1555), who received part of the priory, dissolved by Henry VIII in 1542, as a gift of Catherine Champernowne, of Dartington Hall. His later years were shadowed through the return to Catholic customs during the reign of Queen Mary.

A terra cotta figure of a man reading to a chained prisoner commemorates Walter Venning of Totnes, founder of the Prison Society of Russia, where he died in 1821. The Russian text reads: "I was in prison and you visited me."

One of several famous people baptised here was Dr Benjamin Kennicott, who brilliantly researched the Hebrew text of the Old Testament. He composed the tribute on the tomb of his father, the Parish Clerk and Totnes barber.

In the tower there is a plaque to a Vicar of Totnes and later of nearby Berry Pomeroy, John Prince, author of the invaluable book *The Worthies of Devon.*